MISPLACED PASSION

Poetry to Inspire your Choices

Ebony Brown

Ahzuryte
Books

WHAT DOES YOUR HEART DESIRE...

**"For where your treasure is,
there will your heart be also."**
-Matthew 6:21 KJV

Misplaced Passion
Poetry to Inspire your Choices

Copyright © 2010 by Ebony Brown
Revised version Copyright © 2019 by Ebony Brown
Revised version Copyright © 2022 by Ebony Brown
All rights reserved.

No part of this publication may be reproduced, stored in a retrieval system, or transmitted in any form or by any means – electronic, photocopy, recording, or otherwise – without the prior written permission of the publisher and author.

Misplaced Passion by Ebony Brown
Ahzuryte Books

ISBN: 978-0-615-37275-4

Showing love and thanks...

To my GOD, the Most High, the Omniscient, Omnipotent, Omnipresent, Infinite Divine Consciousness, the Divine Creator whom likeness and image we are made in.

To my daughter, Dayna , you are amazing, and I love you my princess!!! Always know what I do, I do it for us, but it's in the Most High we must place our trust.

To my parents, Aaron, R.I.P., love and miss you and will continue to treasure your fatherly love and Catherine for raising me to have integrity and work for what I want in life.

To my brother, Derwin for watching out for me growing up on the south side of Chicago.

To my cousin, Cathy, R.I.P., miss you and will continue to celebrate the memories of the joyful energy that you freely gave.

Of course to all my family and friends, who have had my back and supported me through my ups and downs. You all know who you are...

"This is to all those who are trying to figure it out...
Stuck in a world full of lies, confusion, and doubt.
Just know things are not always what they seem...
Stay focused on the will of God and you will find your true destiny."
-Ebony Brown

"Wherefore be ye not unwise, but understanding what the will of the Lord is."
-Ephesians 5:17 KJV

"You need to persevere so that when you have done the will of God, you will receive what He has promised"
-Hebrews 10:36 NIV

"Thy kingdom come. Thy will be done in earth, as it is in heaven."
-Matthew 6:10 KJV

Table of Contents

From the Author...xi
Intro...13
Choices..15
Truth I Seek...17
Find It..19
Upgrade or Settle...21
I'm Focused, I'm Centered................................23
Curiosity..25
God is my Judge..27
Ambitious..29
Courageous...31
Dream Again...33
Butterflies...35
I confess...37
Believe in Yourself..39
My heart beats...41
Misunderstood..43
Deep into my Soul..45
Unsure..47
Temporary Insanity..49
Don't Take it Personal....................................53
Spiritual Connection.......................................55
Will you listen..57
No Doubt..59
Be Light as a Feather.....................................61
I'm Free..63
Imagine...65
Priceless..67
God is watching..69

Get yours..71
Questions to think about..73
Outro..75
Bonus: I'm a goddess..77

From the Author

Misplaced Passion is a collection of poetry to inspire you to think about your choices. My words come straight from the heart and I hope that my message reaches your heart and gives you something to reflect upon.

About the author – **Ebony Brown**:

I'm a poet also known as Freele Spoken who wants to rock your heart and soul with words to provoke your thoughts. I'm inspired in many ways, but my experiences and what I've learned from these situations are part of my motivation to successfully move to the next level of goals I desire to accomplish. In this book, I lyrically express my thoughts of how I had to rebuild from within to continue the journey of what I'm destined to do, according to the will of God.

"Claim what you desire and continue to pursue, if it aligns with the will of the Most High, it will happen for you."

@freelespoken

"This book of the law shall not depart out of thy mouth, but thou shalt meditate therein day and night, that thou mayest observe to do according to all that is written therein: for then thou shalt make thy way prosperous, and then thou shalt have good success ." -Joshua 1:8 KJV

"We are of God. He who knows God hears us; he who is not of God does not hear us. By this we know the spirit of truth and the spirit of error." -1 John 4:6 NKJV

"I said, You are gods, And all of you are children of the Most High." -Psalm 82:6 NKJV

"I am a daughter of the Most High"

Intro

Ebony Brown aka Freele Spoken
Here to make you think
About your choices
I choose to speak life
Live life abundantly

I'm a warrior, that's my claim to fame
Will speak my mind
No more do I blame
Now on this spiritual journey, forever learning
Want the same for you, get the Spirit of truth flowing

Hear these words, can you see the passion
Not the bling, but my thoughts I'm flashing!

Choices

Choices, hard to face the reality
Just try trading places with me
My thoughts will make your heart bleed

One step away from going insane
Get on my knees begin to pray
Hands folded
Eyes closed
Where do I begin...

Dear God,
How did I get caught up in this life of confusion...
Not saying I didn't know right from wrong
Only trying to figure out where do I belong
So, now I'm ready to listen...

My child,
This is only the beginning
Your path that you have chosen
Has heightened your reasoning
It may seem foggy, you may not quite understand
But I never left your side
It was you who made the choice to take My hand

Poetry to Inspire your Choices

But God,
Why did You choose me?
I'm the least that people will believe

My child,
Oh please, why can't you see?
It's because of your heart's desire
To truly seek and find Me

Misplaced Passion

Truth I Seek

How did this passion
I was born with go away
It didn't leave
It's still here
It just got misplaced

No longer phony, who you are will be revealed
As a man thinketh, as a man will
Stand up, be who you are
The world is waiting
For your sparkle, shine so bright

The glow is all around you
It's called favor
Starring Leroy, The Last Dragon
Sho nuff, he won the fight
Still standing, still here

Only God can breath into you, eternal life,
No longer in fear
Of what God has for me
Embrace, deeper
It's right there

Poetry to Inspire your Choices

My heart skipped a beat, because I already won
On my path of self realization
Through prayer and meditation
God reveals wisdom and clarification
For me constantly
It's truth I seek

Find It

As I set my eyes forward
Head for the hills
I begin on my mission
Full of life full of thrills

As I pursue the thoughts of my imagination
I become entangled with bliss
Begin to question myself
Could this be a hit or will I miss?

As I take a stroll back down memory lane
When I didn't appreciate the little things
Still wondering
What the future brings

Waiting to release every dream
That takes place
Not sure if it's worth the risk
Not sure if it's worth the wait

We all have a gift
Some people are born with it
Sometimes we have to work it

Poetry to Inspire your Choices

Dreams of your heart can come true
Just remember
Put God first and then do you

Misplaced Passion

Upgrade or Settle

Not here to steal your thunder
Not here to bring the rain,
But like my ancestors
I'm here to bring change!

I see it, I see you
You want to upgrade
Suppressing the mental, dreams delayed
How can I, how do I
Reach the stars
The answer is before you
It's not that hard

To take the first step
Let go of regret
And in your next breath
Ask, what is my gift?

My heart now open
To bring forth to my vision the master plan
Guiding my steps
To upgrade my thought process

Poetry to Inspire your Choices

I know the purpose for my life will come to pass
Choices that I make may determine how fast
God's plan for my life will manifest
Soon as I stop settling for less

So, pioneers, barrier breakers
Continue to come forth
Map out the blue print of success
On how to move forward
Upgrade or settle
The choice is yours

Misplaced Passion

I'm Focused, I'm Centered

I sing with my words
I'm focused, I'm centered
Didn't know pen to pad could paint such a vivid picture

This is nothing new
Just carrying the torch
From the path of those that came before
Blazing a new path for the next generation
To come forth

With wisdom and knowledge
Want you to see
Greater is the Spirit of truth within me

Thank God for sending your messengers for me to see
Examples of how our ancestors built dynasties
Despite the downfall of ancient majesty
Their energy still lives
And it's up to us to continue their legacy

As this path of knowledge continues to unfold
I've learned of the many lies that have been told
Got me looking for my original mindset to be restored

Poetry to Inspire your Choices

I began to uncover the ancestors' stories
Learned of the gods and goddesses, heroes and sheroes
That stood for truth, justice, and morality
So let's continue the movement to this universal order
As we continue to pass knowledge, wealth, and wisdom to our sons and daughters
We continue to learn from our ancestors' business models
That we use to teach our children what to follow
Let's uplift one another to reach our highest potential
To build more empires, constantly creating
Because I know God's got my back and won't keep me waiting

I'm focused, I'm centered

Curiosity

Going, going, I'm gone, ready to do my own thing
Curiosity, it does bring
New thoughts of what I could be
If the destiny I seek chooses me

Still trying to fill a void
Completely annoyed
By what was in my heart
Now more confused
So where do I start

Begin to accept the bad choices
Trust that all is not lost
Take a look at how I perceive things
How I see things
Need to make an adjustment on my thinking

So now what's next
Let go of the foolishness
Stop it at the door
Let my heart explore
Positive thoughts of what God destined me to be
Curiosity does not have to get the best of me

Misplaced Passion

God is my Judge

You have no idea, you have no clue
Don't judge me until you walk in my shoes
What if you thought your last choice was to be a prostitute

Not talking about selling my body for money
I'm talking about letting negativity pimp my mind
And keep me wondering
About the past and all the bad choices I made
I know now the past is what made me who I am today
No longer dying inside

So strong, so sincere
God is my judge
No longer in fear
Of the bondage in my mind
As I've learned is a battlefield

Of Universal Good and Universal Evil
I choose positivity, it's negativity that I'm leaving
Evil forces may try to knock me off my path
But I'm hard to break
So their hold will not last
I continue to walk this infinite path of many lessons
where I work towards attracting heavenly blessings

Ambitious

So you see the images on TV
And begin to wonder and daydream
The glitter, the glamour, and the bling
Maybe you just want to be seen
Just remember there is a price for everything

But don't get it twisted
I'm glad you're ambitious
Stay focused and patient
Keep your mind uplifted

Don't want you to fall from the top of the mountain
Walk down gracefully and move to the next one
God's Spirit within you is there to guide you
While you go through the maze of life
Learning what you are destined to do
You can attain the dreams your heart desires to pursue
When you operate in the gift God gave you
You may see others and think that should be me
But God gave you something special
No need to be
Someone else, you were created uniquely

Poetry to Inspire your Choices

One thing I have learned
There is always a higher place that I may want to go
But now I know
If the peace of God is not in it
It's not worth my soul

Courageous

If you got it all figured out
The words I speak are a waste
Got to move this message to those
Who are ready to embrace
What cannot be seen by the naked eye
A mindset that sees past the myths and lies

To those who want to overcome obstacles
The giants that stand in their way
Nobody can take the gift God gave you
Use it to create opportunities
Which will inspire others to do the same

Look at our ancestors, so courageous
That came before you and me
Harriet Tubman escaped abusive treatment during slavery
and led others through the underground railroad that
desired to be free
Maya Angelou built up self-esteem
Dr. King dared you to dream

From these lessons you must see
Through the power of God
I will fulfill the plans that are destined for me to achieve

Dream Again

It's a beautiful thing
God allows us a choice
Which is not forced
How you will choose
So when you discover who you are
The open door to go through
Is totally up to you

God is so faithful
Allows us to achieve the unthinkable
Not holding back
Moving forward
Please believe it's reachable

No matter what has stopped your reign
The cycle of life does not refrain
You from your chance to begin to dream again

For the dreams planted will come true
According to God's perfect plan
Exclusively for you

Misplaced Passion

Butterflies

I have this feeling
Never felt this before
Nervous energy
What was in store

I think this is serious
I just can't replace
The feeling I had
Butterflies, they wouldn't go away

Developing into something
That would bring so much joy
I'm not sure if I'm ready
Responsibility, will it be a boy or a girl
But this was destined and I'm glad God chose me

To experience this kind of love
I desire to be
An example for my new seed

Will teach her what I now know
Watering her thoughts, now watch her grow
Pure, kind, and true
She will be faithful

Poetry to Inspire your Choices

To who she is, I speak it now
Cause this crazy world
May attempt to turn her out

But as long as I'm here
She will know the truth
About the Spirit of God
Which will not forsake you

Misplaced Passion

I confess

When my halo is off my words are vicious
These scary cats, I make black cats superstitious

Sometimes I'm quick to criticize
I couldn't see it, my own demise
Not saying this for my health
Be careful not to exalt yourself

No harm done
Now know better
Too critical of someone else
You may get the lesson

Humbling experiences
Roles now reversed
Humble now
Kicked off my high horse

These words, I am speaking to those
Who really believe they are untouchable
I'm guilty
Speaking from experience
I never knew, I can't believe I just admitted it
Confessions of a critical mouth

Poetry to Inspire your Choices

Think about what you say
You may lift someone out
Help change their mindset to think more positive

Not to say you can't keep it real
Reality is a must
It's in how you say it
You may have to earn their trust

Oh, I still speak freely
Just not a scavenger
Don't get mad at me
I'm just a messenger

Believe in Yourself

I'm talking to the lost
The scared, the confused, the clueless
You are talented, gifted
You just don't know what to do with it

My message so clear, so concise
Let the Spirit of God begin to raise your consciousness

It's your choice not mine
To seek God's greatness
Be the one like Neo from the Matrix
Have faith to stop bullets
With weapons not of this world

Have you read the art of war?
It's a mindset
Can you see past the here and now?
The temporary wealth
That keeps you running around
Chasing your tail
Because nobody told you the truth
Believe in yourself
Seek the power of God within you

Poetry to Inspire your Choices

It's the Most High you must trust
Time to release from within
Before you bust
Please stop your fronting

Misplaced Passion

My heart beats

Broken, pieces, my heart everywhere
The love I once desired
No longer there
Tried to ignore, what I refused to see
Actions without love so apparent
How could this be

Just wanted your heart to pump for me
The way it pumped when you heard a hot beat
But looking back I kind of see
How my heart may have not been ready to receive
The bigger picture that would connect our dreams

But, yet I kept hearing
My soul telling me it's time to go
But how do I let go of all I'd ever known

How could something so simple
Be so complicated
I saw a flash
What we had to do
I truly hated
We knew we had to say it

Poetry to Inspire your Choices

The last goodbye, so we could be on our way and
Thought I had it figured out
Thought I knew what love was all about

Everything has its purpose in time
No need to rewind
So we could find, so we could see
On separate paths, what love could really be

Thank God for restoration
Mended my heart, so grateful
Keep me busy, my new life has begun
Cares of the world, no longer a burden
Begin to write this poetry
The thoughts I have must be released
For those who may need this therapy

Remember life can still be sweet
Oh yes, prayer changes things
Help find that inner peace
Even at a whisper
You can still hear my heart beats

Misunderstood

I'm in distress
So dysfunctional
Not at my best
Still trying to carry this load

Waiting on my pot of gold
At the end of the rainbow
After the storm, I'm still holding on
Now the sky is so clear
The clouds over me has disappeared

Now you can see the Spirit of God in me
Leading me to my destiny
Knowing my self worth
Redefining my reality

And when things begin to click
Here come the distractions
To hinder my thinking
Attempting to sway my judgment

If I react in anger to the foolishness
The effect will cause me to suffer the consequence

Poetry to Inspire your Choices

So I'm conflicted with thoughts within
Should I express what I feel?
Or hold it in

Not sure how I will be received
Cause when I'm misunderstood
It leads to misunderstandings

Which cause confusion and hate
Attempting to adjust my fate
Learned to not let outside forces trying to manipulate
My path that is destined for me to be great

Will have to distance myself
From those that enjoy seeing others in distress
So, not worried about those who reject
The ideas that I choose to express
Will connect with those
That want to build genuine relationships

Deep into my Soul

Go deep, deep into my soul
It's stimulating
I almost lose control
When our thoughts intertwine
I thought I'd never find
Something so sweet

And no I'm not talking between the sheets
A mental connection, another kind of soul tie
A new joy, a new peace
This new love does not deny

A bond like no other
The power of love is within me
Learning to love myself unconditionally

Seeking that spiritual male warrior type energy
That will complement what defines my inner being
Have your way with my thoughts
So from this dream when I awake
I know I will find the man
Who will understand
That he is my soul mate

Poetry to Inspire your Choices

We both will know it
Will try not to blow it
The chance to romance the fantasy
Of reading each other though mental telepathy
To be continued ...I shall see
If he has what it takes to keep it interesting

Misplaced Passion

Unsure

Please wait a minute
Hold up
It's all too much, my flesh
It's calling
It's so tempting
Now I'm thinking

Is this something I should do?
Doubt, questions, how will I choose
Proceed to go on even though I am in denial

Now have to deal with more tribulations and trials
Added to what was already there, so unnecessary
Heart in motion how will I get out of this
Left in the dark, this nightmare I want to bury

Going in circles, can't sit still
Who can I talk to, who will keep it real
Life can get crazy when I misuse free will

Food for thought that's what this is
Just trust that free will is nothing to play with
Because even with good intentions
There were situations

Poetry to Inspire your Choices

That I was not cautious about my decisions
The moral of this abstract story
Seek God for yourself
If you are unsure about your choices

Temporary Insanity

Coming from the windy city CHI
Landed out in H-town will they treat me right
On this road map of life
Gotta choose your friends right
Because backstabbers, dreamtakers
What I know as common haters
Tried me during trying times
Bamboozled by my foes
Telling pretty little lies

Let me tell you what happened to me
This individual
Took my kindness for weakness
And invaded my privacy

Not your typical foolishness
So get ready for this
A female from the CHI
Far from a hoodrat chick
But still a piece of me on that hood mentality
But in this situation I have to plead temporary insanity

But let me back up explain a few things
I was on a path to change the way I do things

Poetry to Inspire your Choices

Trying out this thing called humility
But I crossed into what I call stupidity
So moving forward, I'm at my place of business
Minding my own
When these haters was all up in my zone
Watching my next move so they could get on
They tried to knock me off my square
But my God wouldn't allow it probably didn't seem fair
Oh there is one detail I have to reveal
One hating female smelled like she took a shower in a landfill
It would be polite to just simply say that she stank
When she walked pass I wanted to walk the plank
But instead of jumping I prayed
While I'm praying everybody spraying
Freesia, Lysol, anything they could get their hands on
Oh and she look like Restputia from Norbit
How you doing
She came to work like soap was an option
I could go on and on
But you all I gotta stop this
So let's get back to the story at hand
Remember I'm minding my own
But haters want to know what turns me on
Why I'm not joining in all they foolishness
I tried to explain my relationship with my God above
But nobody believed I could be that good

Misplaced Passion

So she must be gay being nice to the fishy girl and won't come out and play
Far from that, waiting on my king to arrive to get it right
Good conversation by day, honeymooning by night
So let me shorten this up and get to the point
How my haters set me up
To have the hygiene challenged female ask to use my phone
She downloaded software to track my zones
My phone conversations recorded
Where I'm at, my every move
So, what would make her take the risk
Of losing her job, if I was able to get justice
But then I was hit with the reality
Of how did I let stupidity get the best of me
Oh that's right, I'm claiming temporary insanity
Crazy how this situation was revealed to me
That these people wanted to know me so bad
That they would tap my phone
When I told them the truth when they asked

This right here almost made me lose my mind
But the Universal God showed me everything will be fine
What I mean is there is something called reciprocity
The wrong that they did to me will replay in their lives eventually
So my spirit guides warned to not let my heart grow cold and let the universal law deal with how my enemies' karma will unfold

Don't Take it Personal

They say don't take it personal
But I'm going to take it personal
Loading up this arsenal
Of spoken word, hot verses yo
You all just don't know
How deep this pain here go
But let me please explain
How foolishness will drain
Your energy weakening your strength to lead
Unnecessary jealousy
Let's build up our communities
Unionize our minds to see
How relevant our skills can be

So yeah I take it personal
When I see individuals
With the skills to build
Reconstruction zones up
We don't need another cheer
Just leaders of a different kind
Can't do it alone, it's time to grind
Got to have each other's back
Collectively we shine

Poetry to Inspire your Choices

So you may say FreeleSpoken what you doing about it
I'm just a mouthpiece for those who may be going around it
This subject of how to get ahead
Motivating those whose spirit is dead
I've been there once before won't do it again
So I won't take it personal
Because right now all I'm about to do is win

Will you listen

He hears your prayers
She hears your cries
He knows your heart
She even knows the lies
That have been told against you
Just trust He knows the truth

You are searching for something
That may be missing
Let me slow down
Make sure you get this

When you pray
Do you take a moment to listen?
Some may call it meditation
I simply call it waiting
For the answers, they do come

The human eye just can't see
What the One Most High, does supernaturally
While you wait, fill your thoughts with positivity
As you walk your path of infinite possibilities
That will unfold your heart's desire toward your destiny

Misplaced Passion

No Doubt

On the back burner long enough
Now it's my turn, you live hoping you learn
The lessons of life, that leaves you to question

No longer in doubt
To spread the message
Of what I learned from my mistakes
While going through this journey called life
Each lesson will raise the stakes
But with the right attitude I will not lose

Have to use discernment
Respect those that earn it
Watch out for frenemies
Will set you back from your destiny
Still won't let my haters get the best of me
Won't allow the negative energy to consume me
No weapons formed will prosper against me

Because it's one thing I know, you reap what you sow
Karma can be good or out of control
Your heart will lead you in various ways
You have to decide which side you will play

Misplaced Passion

Be Light as a Feather

Driven by life and all I thought was right
Wanting to fulfill my purpose
Seeking deeper within myself
Waiting for that golden moment

But then I learned of the goddess Maat
Divine principles of Ancient Kemet
She didn't hold back
She embodied morals and values
That kept societies in check
Through her energy
She released the knowledge for the people
To understand this spirituality
Of what is good to uplift humanity

So what about the opposite called Isfet
That turns away from the laws of Maat
God gives us a choice to find the right balance
Gotta learn the rules to understand the challenges

We all have different paths
Some of us may desire to change
Move around
Get in another lane
But like Maat to judge between wrong and right
Every heart will be judged
Based on how each lived their life

Poetry to Inspire your Choices

It will be determined if you walked in truth and righteousness
Your life choices will determine if you reap the rewards or suffer the consequences
So take heed to the warning towards repentance
where these confessions are admittance
Of any wrongs that you may have committed
The choice is ultimately up to you
Either ignore divine law and order
or be obedient and follow through
with principles that will prepare you
for a life that will bring peace and harmony
But, when situations bring the dark cloud of stormy weather
Don't let your heart get to heavy
Continue to make peace with yourself
And be light as a feather

I'm Free

Speak these words
As though they are
Then be courageous
Ignite the spark
Heart start pumping
Adrenaline rush
No longer holding it in
Not a rapper, but rhymes I bust

These words uncensored
Cut your thoughts, I'm blade
No more deception
No longer a slave
To material things of the world
I'm free
Though they slay me
I trust you God
It's just You and me

Imagine

I'm so still, I'm silent
Imagine a world without violence
Almost surreal
Cut the deck
It's time to deal

Who is really winning
Thoughts about the game my head is spinning
Lights out
Eyes open
Let me show you a world about real living
I dare you to take a step
Into to the other side
Over here you don't have to ride the sidelines

It's open you just didn't know you always had the key
I know it may be scary because now you can see
Everybody's hand and how they have been playing
You can now see the card that will be played before it hits the table

Just pay attention and listen to the whispers
It's not what you think, you're just being pushed beyond your limits

Spiritual Connection

I'm so in tune with this spiritual connection
Every word downloaded is so refreshing
This universal wisdom has answered
several of my thought provoking questions
About the depths of what I see
When I look at my reflection

Thankful to the Most High
For divinely guiding me
To uncover the trail of knowledge
From Ancient History
Reading this information
On a daily basis delivered me
From the negative thoughts of self-destruction,
self-pity, self-hate

Empowered by what my ancestors
brought to the human race
No longer confused about who I am
No longer is my passion misplaced

Priceless

Sometimes I wonder about the past
And those that stayed true to the Most High commands
In the scripture it states to test the spirits
Because their influence
Can have you in the spirit of truth or the spirit of delusion
I've studied and explored the prophets and prophetesses from before
And noticed how they would constantly warn
To not go against the laws of God that were set in stone
Written on our hearts
Those that follow will be set apart
Take note of what I am about to share
how a prophetess named Miriam used her wisdom to spare
The life of her brother Moses from the king of Egypt's snare
to assassinate the Hebrew males born from the womb during the midwives care
Miriam knew she was going against the king's command
but she served the laws of her God and would be protected from the king's hand
Another prophet named Daniel who could reveal the king's dreams
A wise man who stayed faithful to his God's policies
There were magicians, astrologers, and sorcerers that tried
But their access to this mystery was painfully denied
The king appreciated the wisdom that Daniel shared and

increased his leadership over the land
The promotion brought about jealousy from the other leaders Daniel surpassed
Take note that Daniel was not there to compete, but promoted while in exile under another king after his homeland's king suffered defeat
But he still followed the laws of his God in a hostile land
So, Daniel's jealous companions conspired and plotted to discredit him
By establishing a statute that whosoever pray to any God or man besides the king
Be thrown into the lion's den
Daniel understood what was happening
But he continued to pray, three times a day
The king realized that his power had been used against him
But still he had to throw Daniel in the lion's den
The Spirit of the Most High was with Daniel and his life was spared
Because Daniel stayed faithful to his God's commands
I aspire to reach this type of faithfulness
I must tell you the message from this prophet and prophetess is following God's law is priceless

God is watching

Yeah, I touched a dream
But for now I'm chasing reality
No longer do I stop to breathe
Catching every breath
I see you got your eye on me
Holding me down
Molding me now

I'm like royalty without the crown
I'm like still waters
Four Tops said it best
Run deep
What you desire
Is within reach

Trust your instincts
Stop second guessing
Just remember
God is always watching
Whatever happens is a blessing

Misplaced Passion

Get yours

Born into this world of darkness and light
Learning I'm not exempt
From the trials of life
Because when I'm wrong
It still seems so right
Sometimes I'm like loose leaf paper
Looking for something to be my staple
Keep me stable
Learned the true meaning of being faithful

Wanted everything
To fall into place
But timing is key
Have to build a solid base

Want you to get in tune with your spirituality
Know thyself, get your destiny
It's up to you to understand
Your connection to the universal God's energy
Revealing your true heart's desire
and what you are truly passionate about
I'm done talking

PEACE AND I'M OUT!

Misplaced Passion

Questions to think about

What motivates you? _____

What are your goals? _____

What do you treasure most? _____

If you have all the answers figured out, then good for you
But for those that don't know, let the journey begin……

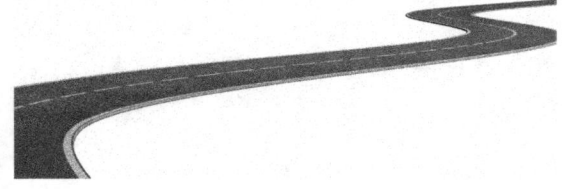

What do you desire and what will you do to get there?

Outro

Freele Spoken in your ear
Here to change the game
Touched by the Spirit of God
No longer the same

It's not about material things
And all it brings
It's about the love of God
It's not about your status
God cares about your heart♥

Misplaced Passion

Bonus: I'm a goddess

Want to know where my power lies
Not saying it's between my thighs
Not saying you won't get a rise
No longer will I compromise
This temple

I'm a goddess
Filled with knowledge
I'm on the edge, but I'm not falling

Thoughts of how I came to be
What if I told you the first human was a she
Created from the dark matter
That gives light through its energy
How on earth did we conceive
Maybe that would be based on what you believe

Studying my roots of Ancient spirituality
When we were referred to as queens
When we crowned our kings to lead
To run major empires, united we have stability

So, ladies we have to get back to our original positions
Like the matriarchs before, to many to mention

Poetry to Inspire your Choices

We have the power, ladies listen
We carry the spiritual prowess
If it's alive, carry on and continue to progress
If it's dormant, time to wake it up, let's do this
I'm here to encourage you and you encourage me
The feminine divine, don't take this gift lightly

I have another point that I would like to make
I know this one may be hard to break
Because there are individuals that may test your attempt to upgrade
May have to let them know that you have no problem with throwing shade
But don't get caught up in the bitter back and forth
Which could lead you to ignore
What you are really here to do
Remember you're a goddess
With spiritual power and greatness
To build nations, our little ones depend on you

So, let's refer to each other as female gods
Also known as queens, instead of female dogs
So, when our men realize they are sons of the Most High
They can come for us as our kings
And together we can overcome any adversity
And continue to build stable families

MISPLACED PASSION
Poetry to Inspire your Choices

Ebony Brown

Ahzuryte Books

"If you do not know where you are going
any road will take you there."
-African Proverb

"There are no limits in God's perfect light to the imagination as you begin to write"

-Ebony Brown

PEACE AND I'M OUT!!!
-aka Freele Spoken

"Therefore you shall love the Lord your God, and keep His charge, and His statutes, and His judgments, and His commandments always."
-Deuteronomy 11:1 NKJV

"Do not think that I came to destroy the Law or the Prophets. I did not come to destroy but to fulfill."
-Matthew 5:17 NKJV

"And one of the elders saith unto me, Weep not: behold, the Lion of the tribe of Judah, the Root of David, hath prevailed to open the book, and to loose the seven seals thereof."
-Revelation 5:5 KJV

www.ingramcontent.com/pod-product-compliance
Lightning Source LLC
Chambersburg PA
CBHW071412290426
44108CB00014B/1795